HEREDITY

HEREDITY
HEREDITY
HEREDITY

HEREDITY

BY ROBERT E. DUNBAR

FRANKLIN WATTS
NEW YORK | LONDON | 1978
A FIRST BOOK

Photographs courtesy of Austrian Information Service: p. 5; Rijksmuseum: pp. 14, 17, 39; U.S. Department of Agriculture, Agricultural Research Service: p. 21 (top and bottom); National Library of Medicine: pp. 28, 31 (left); Pfizer, Inc.: p. 31 (right); United Press International: pp. 41, 47.

Illustration p. 30, adapted from "The Recombinant-DNA Debate" by Clifford Grobstein. Copyright © 1977 by Scientific American, Inc. All rights reserved.

Diagrams, pp. 7, 11, 25, 34, 37, and 50 from Vantage Art, Inc.

Library of Congress Cataloging in Publication Data

Dunbar, Robert E
    Heredity.

    (A First book)
    Includes index.
    SUMMARY: Discusses the research of Mendel and Darwin, cell structure, DNA, mutation, heredity vs. environment, and controlling heredity. Includes projects in these areas, designed for self-discovering genetic principles.
    1. Genetics—Juvenile literature. [1. Genetics] I. Title.
QH437.5.D86   575.1   77–16584
ISBN 0–531–01408–8

Cover design by Nick Krenitsky

CONTENTS

HEREDITY

HEREDITY AND YOU

CHAPTER

1

When you were born, your parents had no idea what you would look like or what you would grow up to be. From the first they have probably studied you to find out exactly who in your family you look like and what abilities you may have inherited.

Think about yourself for a moment. Are you light-haired like your father when he was young? Is your hair curly like your mother's? Are your eyes blue or brown? What shape nose do you think you will have when you grow up? Will you be tall or short? Do you have a talent for music or mathematics? Are you strong and well coordinated, good in sports? Are you a good student in school? Do you learn things easily? Or are you good in some subjects, but not so good in others? Do you like to read books or would you rather be outside exploring the world around you?

All of these traits, and many, many more, are partly a result of your *heredity.* You have inherited many physical traits from your parents and grandparents. Whatever talents and abilities you have shown so far are also due in part to your heredity.

But what about the world around you? How do you think it has affected you? What kind of world do you live in? Do you live in a city, in the country, or in a suburb of a large city? Do you live in an apartment or in a house? Where you live and who you live with are part of your *environment.* So are your friends, your school, your place of worship, the country you live in, the books you read, the movies you see, and the shows you watch on television. All of these things have an influence on who you are.

Heredity is a science. As sciences go, it is a fairly new one, only about a hundred years old. Some other sciences, such as biology, chemistry, medicine, and mathematics, are much older. People have thought about heredity for a long time. But until recently they didn't know much about how it happened or what made it happen.

As you will read, we now know that each of us is the result of many generations of ancestors. Some of the traits you have inherited may have come from your great-great-great-grandparents, who lived more than two hundred years ago!

In the last hundred years we have also discovered a great deal about how environment affects heredity. Many species of plants and animals have died out because they couldn't survive in a particular environment. Others have survived because they inherited traits that helped them to adapt. Humans are a good example. Our hands have made it possible for us to make many things to protect us from the harshness of our environment, and so has our intelligence.

The science of heredity has also taught us much about the great variety of plant and animal life in all living species. Look at all the differences in your friends at school. Hair can be many shades of blonde, brown, or black. Eyes and noses can be quite different. Some people are tall, some are short, and some are in between. And can you think of any-one's voice that sounds exactly like another person's?

In this book you will be finding out about the science of heredity. You will be exploring exactly what heredity is and how it can affect the way you respond to the world you live in, your environment. You will also be finding out how environment can affect heredity. It sounds complicated. But let's start at the beginning, and find out how the science of heredity began.

A MAN CALLED MENDEL

CHAPTER
2

Gregor Johann Mendel is known as the father of the science of heredity. He was born in 1822 in Heinzendorf, a rural community in Austria (now part of Czechoslovakia). As a boy on his father's farm, Gregor became very interested in the plants and animals around him. He liked to study them and try to figure out why some were different from others.

Gregor was brought up in a poor but very religious Roman Catholic family. He was a good student at school and wanted to continue his studies at a university. His parents, however, could not afford the expense. He did have one opportunity to continue his education. This was to become a priest. In those days, becoming a priest meant that a young man could be educated by the church and become a teacher in one of the church schools. This was something that Mendel wanted very much to do. He was deeply religious and knew he would like the life of a priest and teacher.

In 1843, when he was 21 years old, Mendel entered the St. Augustine Monastery in Brunn, Austria. He studied first with

Gregor Mendel

other priests at the monastery and later at the University of Vienna. When he had completed his education, he returned to Brunn and taught science at a high school run by the monastery. He also began to spend more and more time in the study of plants, or botany. In the monastery gardens he experimented with many different kinds of plants. After a time he was given a garden plot of his own in which to continue his experiments. It was in this garden that Mendel began his now famous experiments with garden peas.

Pea plants are *self-pollinating.* That is, each pea plant develops a flower that contains a *stamen,* also called the male part, and a *pistil,* also called the female part. For the plant to reproduce, the stamen releases tiny seeds called *pollen,* which fertilize *eggs* contained in the pistil. When this happens, the plant produces pods filled with peas, or *offspring.* Each pea, when planted, will produce a new plant. When the flower forms, it too will contain both male and female parts capable of producing offspring.

Mendel started with thirty-four varieties of pea plants. Some were tall, some were short. Some had white flowers, others had purple flowers. Some of the seeds the plants produced were yellow, others were green. Some were wrinkled, some were smooth. His purpose was to find out what principles, or basic rules, governed heredity. For example, he wanted to know what made one plant short with purple flowers and another plant tall with white flowers.

Mendel experimented for two years, using a method known as *hybridization.* In hybridization, one or more varieties within a species are *crossed,* or bred together, to produce a new variety. To make this happen, Mendel would remove the stamens, or male parts, to prevent self-pollination. He would then pollinate each plant by hand, using the pollen from another variety. At first he decided to trace only

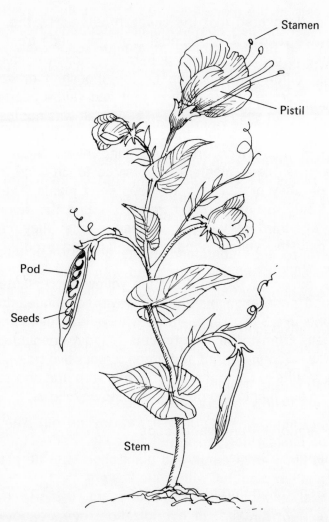

Stamen

Pistil

Pod

Seeds

Stem

one characteristic at a time, such as tallness. Mendel used about a thousand plants in each experiment and kept very detailed records of the results.

In one set of experiments he crossed yellow seed plants with green seed plants by fertilizing the pistils in the yellow seed plant with pollen from the green seed plant, and vice versa. He discovered that the seeds produced by the plants were always yellow. Then Mendel took the seeds from these new plants to grow a second generation. However, this time something different happened. Of the thousand or so new plants, an average of three out of four had yellow seeds! The others had green seeds. The green seed trait was not lost. But it didn't show up again until the second generation.

Mendel also discovered something else. When seeds from the green seed plants were planted to produce a third generation, they produced only green seed plants. They had inherited only the green seed trait. He found the same was true for one-third of the yellow seed plants: they had inherited *only* the yellow seed trait and could produce *only* yellow seed plants.

The remaining two-thirds of the yellow seed plants from the second generation planting, however, continued to produce plants in a 3 to 1 ratio—three with yellow seeds and one with green. From these experiments Mendel concluded that yellow was a *dominant* trait and green a *recessive* trait.

The results of Mendel's experiments with first and second generation pea plants can be diagrammed as follows:

First Generation Parent Plant Seeds		YY	gg	
The "Offspring" Seeds	Yg	Yg	Yg	Yg
Second Generation Parent Plant Seeds		Yg	Yg	
The "Offspring" Seeds	YY	Yg	Yg	gg

In this illustration, *Y* represents the dominant trait of yellow seeds. The *g* stands for the recessive trait of green seeds. Note: The 3 to 1 ratio is an average based on using large numbers of plants. This ratio will not necessarily show up if only a few plants are used in an experiment.

MENDEL'S LAWS

CHAPTER
3

Over the next eight years, Mendel did more and more complex experiments with pea plants. He tried many different combinations and grew many generations of plants. When he was satisfied that he had discovered some basic principles of heredity, he decided to make his discoveries known. His chance came in 1865 at a meeting of the Brunn Society for the Study of Natural Science.

What Mendel had discovered was so new and exciting that he expected to amaze the other scientists and people all over the world. Before the Society, in a strong, clear voice, he stated the following:

(1) That for every trait showing up in a plant, there are two trait "determiners" in the plant's seed. One is inherited from the male part (the stamen) and one from the female part (the pistil). The two determiners can be the same (for example, *gg*) or different (*Yg*).

(2) That in every pair of contrasting traits (for example, yellow/green or tallness/shortness), one will be dominant and one recessive.

(3) That plants which carry only the recessive (or only the dominant) trait determiners (for example, *gg* or *YY*) can produce only plants with that trait.

(4) That the distribution of dominant and recessive traits is determined by chance, but over the long run one can predict the results, according to ratios that he had worked out.

When Mendel was through he waited for the response of amazement. It was not to happen. The scientists didn't seem to realize the importance of his discoveries. Their attention was drawn away by reports about the discoveries of another man, Charles Darwin. It was not until almost a half-century later, long after he had died and been forgotten, that Mendel's work on the laws of heredity was rediscovered and found to be just as true for humans as it was for plants.

FIND-OUT-FOR-YOURSELF Project 1: Using Mendel's method, discover the principles of heredity for yourself. Grow some garden peas. You can get the seeds from a nursery or a large plant store. Choose two varieties that differ in height when fully grown. The Freezonian, Little Marvel, and Greenshaft varieties are good to use. The pods are similar, and all are fully grown in about sixty-three days. The Freezonia and Greenshaft plants grow 30 inches (11.7 cm) tall, but Little Marvel grows only 18 inches (7.02 cm) tall.

1. Select some seeds of the short variety and some of the tall variety. Plant them side by side in two rows, following the instructions on each seed envelope. If planting inside, place the plant container on a windowsill that gets sun most of the day. If planting outside, plant in the spring, after the danger of frost has passed. When the plants begin to appear, keep

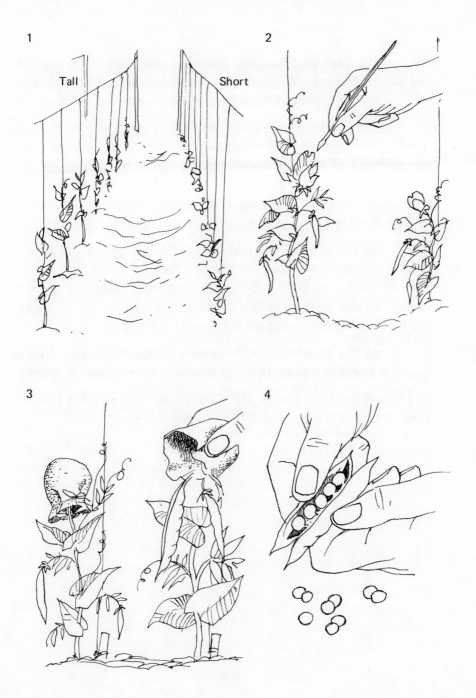

1 Tall   Short

your garden plot well weeded. After several weeks, the flowers will begin to form. When you pry open the buds (step 2), you will see pollen forming on each plant's stamen.

2.   Before the flowers have opened, pry open the buds and remove the stamens with tweezers. Transfer the pollen from the stamens of the tall variety to the tip of the pistils of the short variety. Use a small artist's paintbrush. Then transfer the pollen from the stamens of the short variety to the pistils of the tall variety.

3.   If you have planted outside, gently cover the flower on each plant with a small cloth bag. This is done to prevent it from being fertilized by other sources, such as pollen carried by the wind or by bees. Look in once in a while. When the flowers have developed into pods, remove the cloth bags.

4.   When the plants are fully grown, remove the pea seeds from the pods and plant them to produce a new crop of plants.

5.   When the new plants are fully grown, write down the results. Which is the dominant trait, tallness or shortness?

DARWIN AND EVOLUTION

CHAPTER
4

Like Mendel, Charles Darwin had a great curiosity about the life around him when he was a boy. Born in 1809 in Shrewsbury, England, Darwin lived about the same time as Mendel and like Mendel loved to explore the countryside near his hometown. For enjoyment he also liked to catch rats and do chemical experiments.

Darwin's father, like his father before him, was a well-to-do doctor. His mother was Susannah Wedgwood of the famous Wedgwood pottery and porcelain family. When it came time for Charles to go to college, there was no question about what he would take up: medicine. He was sent to one of the best medical schools of the time, which was located in Edinburgh, Scotland.

Darwin tried to be a good student, but he thought his teachers and the subjects they taught dull. When he saw an operation being performed on a child who was awake, he became sick over the screaming and at the sight of blood. (Anesthesia, or sleeping drugs, had not yet been discovered.)

It was at medical school, however, that Darwin learned about the French scientist Lamarck and his theory of *evolution.* According to this theory, all living things undergo change over long periods of time. Darwin's grandfather, Erasmus Darwin, had also written about evolution. But the theory had not been proved.

Most people of Darwin's day shared the belief that God had created all plant and animal life on earth at the same time, and that there had been no real change since the creation. This was known as the *theory of special creation.* Darwin believed this too. As a hobby, however, he began to collect marine animals and shells and study their similarities and differences. He became deeply fascinated with this study.

At medical school, however, young Charles was a failure. He just couldn't get interested in becoming a doctor. In the hopes he could succeed in becoming a preacher instead, another highly respected profession, Darwin was sent off to study at the University of Cambridge in England.

Darwin's botany teacher at Cambridge was the Reverend John Henslow. Henslow found in Darwin a willing student, and took a special interest in him. Eventually, Henslow recommended Darwin for the job of naturalist (one who studies plant and animal life) on the British ship *H.M.S. Beagle.* The *Beagle* was about to begin a voyage of scientific exploration that would last five years. Darwin had finally found his calling. He happily dropped his pursuit of the priesthood and prepared to begin his new life as a scientist of nature.

Charles Darwin

THE ORIGIN OF SPECIES

CHAPTER
5

The *H.M.S. Beagle* left England in December 1831, with Darwin on board. Thus began a trip that would cover many parts of the world. Most of the time, however, was spent along the coasts of South America and its nearby islands, including the famed Galapagos Islands.

As the ship's naturalist, Darwin collected thousands of specimens of animal and plant life. He studied these very closely and wrote about them in his notebooks. He also wrote about them to other scientists. Most of the specimens were shipped back to England so others could study them too.

Some of the specimens Darwin found were living. He also dug up fossils from deep in the ground where they had been buried for many thousands of years. In the case of animals, fossils usually consist of skeletons or bones. Plant fossils are more often just outlines appearing in mud or sand that has hardened into rock. Studying the different varieties of ancient and living plants and animals, Darwin was able to trace their histories. What amazed him was how certain varieties had developed, or evolved, over time. Some traits had remained, others had been lost, and new traits had appeared.

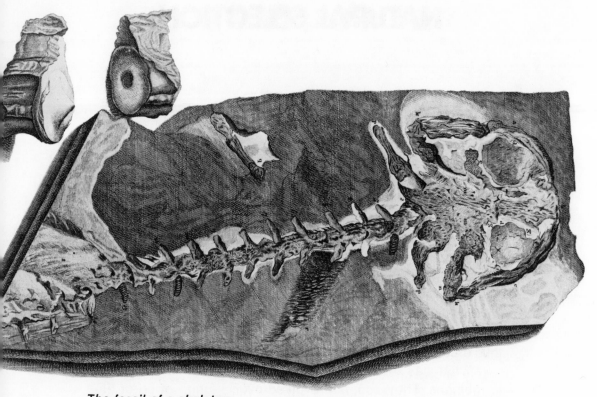

The fossil of a skeleton

The *Beagle* returned to England in October 1836. Darwin continued his studies of plants and animals from his home in England, and began to develop, test, and retest his own theory of evolution. Seventeen years later, in 1859, Darwin published a book, *The Origin of Species,* summarizing his findings. Quite surprisingly to Darwin, the book was an immediate success. In fact, to Darwin's great amazement, his book actually created a storm of reaction throughout the world among scientists and non-scientists alike.

NATURAL SELECTION

CHAPTER
6

When Darwin left for his voyage on the *Beagle,* he still believed in the theory of special creation. But by tracing the ancestors of plant and animal life, he became convinced otherwise. Life on earth *progressed* through evolution. No two plants or animals were exactly alike. *Most* of a species' traits were passed on. But sometimes an entirely new trait would appear, thus creating a new species.

What was true for all plant and animal life was also true for humans. They, too, had evolved over a long period of time from primitive beginnings. What shocked many people was the evolutionary fact that humans were related to other animal life, in particular to mammals, such as the apes, or to apelike humans discovered in fossil remains of many thousands of years ago.

Many of the people who opposed Darwin's ideas on evolution thought he did not believe in God. But Darwin was very religious. He believed in God as the creator of all things. But he believed he had proof that all things created by God were subject to change and that this was part of God's "Divine Plan."

Darwin's most important concept in his theory of evolution he called *natural selection*. Natural selection is basically nature's way of determining *how* plant and animal species change over long periods of time. One aspect of this theory is the idea of the *survival of the fittest*. Each year hundreds of thousands of different animals and plants are born. Many are killed by enemies, disease, or harsh weather conditions. But a certain number usually survive and continue to produce offspring.

In most cases, the plants and animals that survive are the *best fitted* to survive under the conditions in which they live. Some plants become disease-resistant or can withstand long dry spells, heavy flooding, or severe windstorms. The same principle holds true for animals. Those who are faster runners have a better chance of escaping from their enemies. Those with a thick coat of fur to keep them warm in subzero temperatures stay alive. *Variation* among offspring within a species helps increase the chance that that species can adapt to an environment. Offspring with "helpful" traits can pass those traits on.

Many plants and animals have become extinct because they could not survive in a changing environment. For example during the great Ice Age, which began two million years ago, there were periods of intense cold that lasted thousands of years. Most of North America, from the Arctic circle to the Ohio and Missouri river valleys, was covered with ice. So was much of northern England, western Denmark, and Germany. Many plants and animals that were native to those areas were killed off by the ice and severe cold. Some plants, which had spread to areas that were free from ice, were able to survive. The same was true for animals that were able to escape to warmer climates.

Plants and animals that are able to survive and produce

offspring help determine the traits of those who come after them. Darwin called this process *heredity*. Darwin didn't understand exactly how heredity came about. But as was shown earlier, Gregor Mendel was at work at the same time in another place, developing the basic laws that govern heredity.

FIND-OUT-FOR-YOURSELF Project 2: Read about dinosaurs and find out why they became extinct. Then try answering these questions:

1. How did changes in the climate make it impossible for them to find enough food to survive? Were they killed off by their enemies? Did they inherit a fatal disease or become physically weak?
2. What animals now living are probably descendants of the dinosaurs?

Record the results of your study.

FIND-OUT-FOR-YOURSELF Project 3: Ask your parents to take you to an animal breeding farm or experimental nursery. Try to arrange in advance for an interview with the person in charge. Find out how the principles of heredity are used to produce the healthiest and most productive plants or animals.

Here are some questions you can ask about plants:

1. Are you experimenting with plants to make them disease-resistant?

Two plant geneticists. The one above is working to increase the protein content and quality of wheat. The one below is trying out various wheat strains for disease resistence.

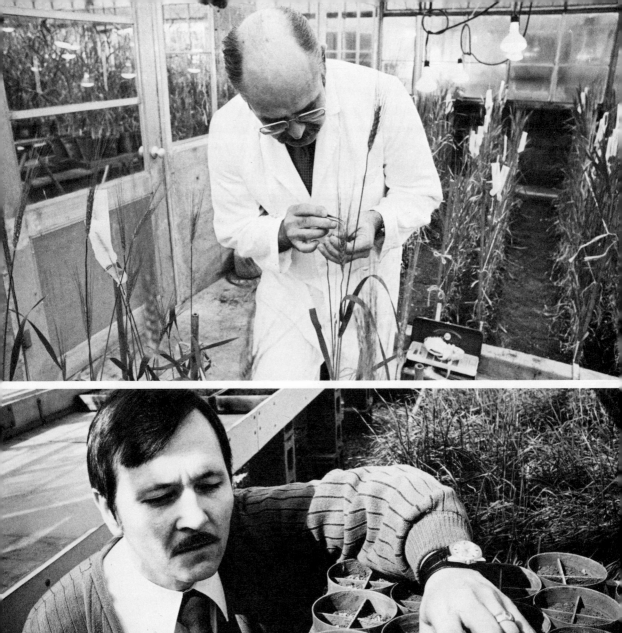

2. What makes a plant disease-resistant or healthier than another plant?
3. How do you develop a plant that is disease-resistant?
4. How long does it take to develop a plant that is disease-resistant?

Here are some questions to ask about animals:

1. Are you developing any new breeds of animals?
2. What traits do you want the new breed to have?
3. How are you developing the new breed?
4. How long will it take for you to develop the new breed?

Record the results of your interview.

CELLS: THE BUILDING BLOCKS OF LIFE

CHAPTER
7

The work of Mendel and Darwin told the world much about the science of heredity and the variations and changes in plants and animals. But without an understanding of the tiny cells that make up all living organisms, we would not be able to know exactly how heredity works.

In 1655 the Englishman Robert Hooke, an inventor and scientist, designed his own microscope so he could have a workable tool with which to magnify small objects. One day when he was experimenting with his new invention, he picked up a small piece of cork, sliced a thin portion of it, and placed it under the microscope's magnifying glass. It surprised him to see that the cork was made up of a series of tiny compartments. He called these compartments *cells,* because of their resemblance to the cells of a honeycomb.

It wasn't until nearly two centuries later, however, that scientists, using an improved microscope to study the structures of plants and animals, realized how important Hooke's discovery was. The credit for this goes to two German scientists, Matthias Schleiden, a botanist, and Theodor Schwann, a zoologist (a scientist who specializes in the study of animals).

Independently of each other and at about the same time, Schleiden discovered that all plants are made up of a series of tiny cells, and Schwann reported the same thing to be true of animals. That same year, 1838, the two men met for the first time and compared notes. When Schwann took Schleiden to his laboratory to examine a section of animal tissue he had been working on, Schleiden was amazed to see how similar plant and animal cells were. The work of these two men led to the *cell theory*, now accepted as fact, which states that all living organisms, plant and animal, are made up of similar tiny structures, called cells, which are the building blocks of life.

CELL STRUCTURE

As a result of the writings of Schleiden and Schwann, scientists became more aware of the importance of cells. New, more powerful microscopes were invented to study them. We now know that every fully grown human being is made up of over 100,000,000,000,000 of these cells!

The cells of animals are a little different from those of plants. Every animal cell has an outer coating to protect it, called the *cell membrane.* Inside the membrane is a substance called *cytoplasm* and a structure called the *nucleus.* The cytoplasm contains mostly water plus a number of tiny structures called *organelles.* The nucleus of a cell is located near the middle and is usually round in shape, with a special covering around it called the *nuclear membrane.* In this nucleus lies the key to heredity.

In all higher forms of life, including humans, there is a division of labor among the cells. That is, groups of cells (such as bone, blood, and skin cells) work together to perform a particular body function. It is the material within the nucleus that "tells" the cell what to do. Even though most cells in an organism contain all the hereditary material, only *some* of the information in each cell is put to use, "turned on."

Some cells, such as blood and skin cells, can reproduce themselves. When you cut your skin, the skin cells around the wound will multiply, and, eventually, you will have new skin. Other types of cells, such as nerve cells, cannot reproduce themselves. If you damage a nerve, a new nerve will not grow back. With aging, all cells begin to lose their ability to reproduce. Sometimes, too, something goes wrong, and the cells *cannot stop* reproducing themselves. This condition is known as cancer.

New cells are produced in both plants and animals by a process called *mitosis,* or cell division. In this process the nuclear material first duplicates itself. Then the cell divides

STAGES OF MITOSIS

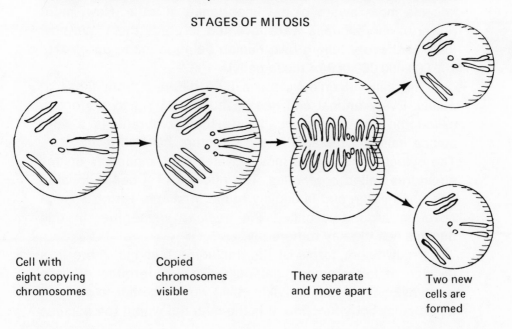

Cell with
eight copying
chromosomes

Copied
chromosomes
visible

They separate
and move apart

Two new
cells are
formed

[25]

to form two identical cells. Each new cell has the same amount of nuclear material the original cell had.

Toward the end of the nineteenth century, scientists discovered that within the nucleus of each cell are smaller units called *chromosomes.* The name chromosome comes from the Greek words *chroma* (color) and *soma* (body). They got this name because they quickly absorb the dyes used by biologists to study them under a microscope. Eventually, scientists realized that even smaller units made up the chromosomes—*genes.* When Mendel's work was rediscovered in the early 1900s, it all fell together: the units, or trait determiners that Mendel had referred to, were genes. Within each chromosome could be found many genes arranged in a very exact order or pattern.

YOU AND YOUR GENETIC CODE

CHAPTER
8

Long before scientists discovered that genes control heredity, they knew that the chromosomes in each cell were made up of protein and a special chemical material called deoxyribonucleic (dee OK see ri bo noo CLAY ik) acid, commonly known as *DNA.* Even though all cells have specific individual functions, such as to grow hair, bone, or muscle, almost every cell has the same amount and type of DNA.

DNA had first been discovered in 1869 by a Swiss chemist, Friedrich Miescher. At the time, however, scientists didn't think DNA was very important. But in 1944, the Rockefeller Institute in New York City, under the direction of Oswald T. Avery, announced that DNA, and DNA alone, was the substance responsible for heredity. A little earlier than that two American scientists, George W. Beadle and Edward L. Tatum, had discovered that genes, which make up DNA, control the production of *enzymes.* Enzymes are proteins that speed up all chemical reactions in the body, such as turning food to fuel. Thus, genes may supply answers to questions such as what makes all life and growth possible. With these discoveries came the first major attempts to decipher the *genetic code.*

But what is the genetic code?

DNA is usually found in a very long double strand, made up of a series of genes or units, also known as *nucleotides,* that are attached to each other. The two strands carry genetic information (nose shape, height, etc.) They are arranged so that different units are opposite each other. It is always the same pair of units that are opposite each other in a normal human being.

Let's take two pairs of units, for example, and call them A and T, G and C.* Wherever A appears on one strand, T will appear opposite it on the other strand. The same goes for the G and C units. Here is an example of a double strand of DNA that contains nine pairs of these units:

A Sample Strand of DNA Containing Nine Units
And the Double Strand Formed by their Pairing

ATTAGACAA
TAATCTGTT

In a single human cell, DNA is made up of about 6,000,000,000 units! It is usually found in the form of a very long, unbroken thread.

In 1953 two scientists, Francis H. C. Crick from Britain and James D. Watson from the United States, made a model of the DNA molecule. This is the tiniest part of the DNA substance containing all the properties of DNA. It is only a

* Actually, these letters stand for the four nucleotides—adenine, thymine, guanine, and cytosine—that make up the double-strand DNA molecule.

Frederick Miescher

```
GAGTTTTATCGCTTCCATGACGCAGAAGTTAACACTTTCGGATATTTCTGATGAGTCGAAAAATTATCTTGATAAACGAGGAATTACTACTGCTTGTTTA
TCAACTACCGCTTTCCAGCGTTTCATTCTCGAAGAGCTCGACGCGTTCCTATCCAGCTTAAAAGAGTAAAAGGCGGTCGTCAGGTGAAGCTAAATTAAGC
AACGATTCTGTCAAAAACTGACGCGTTGGATGAGGAGAAGTGGCTTAATATGCTTGGCACGTTCGTCAAGGACTGGTTTAGATATGAGTCACATTTTGTT
TGAACTGAGTACTAAAGAATGGATAATCACCAACTTGTCGTAGCCTGAGTCTATCATTAGGTGCGAGAAAATTTTACAGTTGTTCTCTTAGAGATGGTAC
TACTGAACAATCCGTACGTTTCCAGACCGCTTTGGGCTCTATTAAGCTCATTCAGGCTTCTGCCGTTTTGGATTTAACCGAAGATGATTTCAGTTTTCTG
TCGCTTCCCATAGGATGTTTCAGGTCGACTGGTATTTGCGTTCGGAGTTGCGTCGCTGCTCGTGCTCTCGCCAGTCATCGTTAGGTTTGAAACAATGAGCA
TTCCTGCTCCTGTTGAGTTTATTGCTGCCGTCATTGCTTATTATGTTCATCCCGTCAACATTCAAACGGCCTGTCTCATCATGGAAGGCGCTGAATTTAC
CAGTCATTCTTGCAGTCACAAAGGACGVGCAGTTGCGTTCCATTTGCCGCTTGTTAAGTCGCCGAAATTGGCCTGCGAGCTGCGGTAATTATTACAAAAGG
GCAGAAGAAAAGCTGCGTCAAAAATTACGTGCGGAAGGAGTGATGTAATGTCTAAAGGTAAAAAACGTTCTGGCGCTCGCCCTGGTCGTCCGCACGCCGTT
TTAAATAGGAGTTCATTCCCCGGCTTCGGGGACGTTAATTTTAACAACTGGTGGATGTATGGTTTCTGCTCGCGGAAATGCGAACGGAAATCATGGAGCG
ATGTCTAATTATCAACTGGCGCCGAGCGTATGCCGCATGACCTTTCCCATCTTGGCTTCCTTGCTGGTCAGATTGGTCGTCTTATTACCATTTCAACTA
TACAGATGTCATCTCAGTTATCGTTGCGGTGCTGCGTTACCTCTTTCTGCCTCTCGCGGTTGCCGCAGGTAGAGCTTCCTCAGCGGTCGCTATTGGCCTG
TTTTACTTTTTATGTCCCTCATCGTCAGCTTTATGGTGAACAGTGGATTAAGTTCATGAAGGATGGTGTTAATGCCACTCCTCTCCCGACTGTTAACCAA
GATATCTATAGTTTATTGGGACTTTGTTTACGAATCCCTAAAATAACCATAGTCCCAATTAGCACGGTTCTTTTCGCCGTACCAGTTATATTGGTCATCA
CGTATTTTAAACCGCCGTGG--ATGCCTGACCGTACCAGGCTAAACCTAATGAGCTTAATCAAGATGATGCTCGTTATGGTTTCCGTTGCCACCATCT
TCGTCGAACGTCTGGGTATTACAGTTATCTACACCATCTTCAGCAGTAAACCGCTCTTTCGAGTCAGAGTCCTCCTTCGGCTCGTCGTCAGGTTTACAAAAC
TATGCTAATTTGCATACTGACCAAGAACGTCGATTACTTCATGCAGCGTTACCATGA-GTTATTTCTTCATTTGGAGGTAAAACCTCATATGACGCTGACA
ACTTGTGCTGGTCTTTTGACCGGATTGCTGCAAACCAGTCAAGGTAGTTGTAGTATCGGTCTACGGGTCTCTAATCTCGCGTACTGTTCATTTCCTGCCA
ACAGACCTATAAACATTCTGTGCCGCGTTTCTTTGTTCCTGAGCATGGCACTATGTTTACTCTTGCGCTTGGTTCGTTTTCCGCCTACTGCGACTAAAGAG
GGAAGTATCTTTAAAGTGCGCCGCCGTTCAACGGTATGTTTGTCCCAGCGGTCGTTATAGCGCATATTCAGTTTCGTGGAAATCGCAATTCCATGACTTA
ATGTTTTCCGTTCTGGTGATTCGTCTAAGAAGTTTAAGATTGCTGAGGGTCAGTGGTATCGTTATGCGCCTTCGTATGTTTCTCCTGCTTATCACCTTCT
TTGACTTGCTGACTTTGTGACCAGTATTAGTACCAACGCTTATTCATGCGCAAGAACGTTTAGTTGTCTTCCGCCAAGGACTTACTTACCCTTCGGAAGT
GTTGCAGTGGATAGTCTTACCTCATGTGACGTTTATCGCAATCTGCCGACCACTCGCGATTCAATCATGACTTCGTGATAAAGATTGAGTGTGAGGTTA
TTTCAGACTTTGTACTAATTTGAGGATTCGTCTTTTGGATGGCGCGAAGCGAACCAGTTGGGGAGTCGCCGTTTTTAATTTTAAAAATGGCGAAGCCAAT
TATTTCTCGCCACAATTCAAACTTTTTTTTCTGATAAGCTGGTTCTCACTTCTGTTACTCCAGCTTCTTCGGCACCTGTTTTACAGACACCTAAAGCTACA
GGACTAATCGCCGCAACTGTCTACATAGGTAGACTTACGTTACTTCTTTTGGTGGTAATGGTCGTAATTGGCAGTTTGATAGTTTTATATTGCAACTGCT
TTGTTTCAGTTGGTGCTGATATTGCTTTTGATGCCGACCCTAAATTTTTTGCCTGTTTGGTTCGCTTTGAGTCTTCTTCGGTTCCGACTACCCTCCCGAC
TAACGGCCCGCATGCCCCTTCCTGCAGTTATCAGTGTGTCAGGAACTGCCATATTATTGGTGGTAGTACCGCTGGTAGGTTTCCTATTTGTAGTATCCGT
AACGTCTACGTTGGTTTCATGGTTTGGTCTAACTTTACCGCTACTAAATGCCGCGGATTGGTTTCGCTGAATCAGGTTATTAAAGAGATTATTTGTCTCC
AACTGGCGGAGGTTTGTTAAATCTGTACCGCGGTGGTCGTTCTCGTCTTCGTTATGGCGGTCGTTATCGTGGTTTGTATTTAGTGGAGTGAATTCACCGA
AAAGCCGCCTCCGGTGGCATTCAAGGTGATGTGCTTGCTACCGATAACAATACTTGAGGCATGGGTGATGCTGGTATTAAATCTGCCATTCAAGGGCTTCA
CTTCACGGTCGGACGTTGCATGGAAGTTCTTCAGGAAATGGTCGAAATCGTTATCGTGTCCTTTGTTTTGATCCCCGCCGGAGTAGTCCCAATCCTTGTA
TGCCGTTTCTGATAAGTTGCTTGATTTGGTTGGACTTGGTGGCAAGTCTGCCGCTGATAAAGGAAAGGATACTCGTGATTATCTTCGTGCTGCATTTCCT
GGTCAACGTAAAATCATTCGAGAAAAACTAAGAGTTTAGGCCGCAGTTGGTATGGTCGGCTCCTTCGTAGTCGTGGTCGTGCGAGGGTTCGTAATTCGA
ACAATCAGAAAGAGATTGCCGAGATGCAAAATGAGACTCAAAAAGAGATTGCTGGCATTCAGTCGGCGACTTCACGCCAGAATACGAAAGACCAGGTATA
CCTTTGGACGACAACGAACCTTTCTAACCACAAAAGGTATTATCTGCGTTGCGTCGTCATCTGAGGAAGACA-CTTATTCGTTCGTAGAGTAAAACACGT
GAGATTATGCGCCAAATGCTTACTCAAGCTCAAACGGCTGGTCAGTATTTTACCAATGACCAAATCAAAGAAATGACTCGCAAGGTTAGTGCTGAGTTG
GGTCTTCGTCGTAGTCACTGCTGTAATCTTTATAGGAAACGTCATCGCGGTTATACTCTTCGGTATGGCGACTAAGACGCAAACGACTACTTGATTCA
TGTGGTTGATATTTTTCATGGTATTGATAAAGCTGTTGCCGATACTTGGAACAATTTCTGGAAAGACGGTAAAGCTGATGGTATTGGCTCTAATTTGTCT
TAAGTCTTCCCATTATTCTTGCTTGGTATTTTTTCGGAGGTTCTAAACCTCCGTACTTTTGTATGTTAACCCTCCCACAGTTAGGACTGCCAATAAAGGA
GTCACGCTGATTATTTTGACTTTGAGCGTATCGAGGCTCTTAAACCTGCTATTGAGGCTTGTGGCATTTCTACTCTTTCTCAATCCCCAATGCTTGGCTT
CGGCAGTTGTATGTATAGTGGTAATAGCTTGAGTTGCGGGACGTATGCTTTTCTGTCTTAGAGAAGGTTCTCGAACTACGCCAATAGGTAGACGAATACC
CATAAGGCTGCTTCTGACGTTCGTGATGAGTTTGTATCTGTTACTGAGAAGTTAATGGATGAATTGGCACAATGCTACAATGTGCTCCCCCAACTTGATA
CCCGCAAGTCGTCGGTCGAACGTTTGACGCATTGGCAGAGAGCAAGAGATTTTTGGTAAAAAGCAGGGGAAGCCCCGCCACCAGATATCACAATAATT
TCTTAAGGATATTCGCGATGAGTATAATTACCCCAAAAAGAAAGGTATTAAGGATGAGTGTTCAAGATTGCTGGAGGCCTCCACTAAGATATCGCGTAGA
GATTAGCCAGCAGTCGGTTGCACTCTCACAGTTTTGCTATTTGGTTGGTAGTCGTACTCGGACAGCGTAACGTAAGTAGTTTGCGACTTATCGTTTCGG
AGGCGTTTTATGATAATCCCAATGCTTTGCGTGACTATTTTCGTGATATTGGTCGTATGGTTCTTGCTGCCGAGGGTCGCAAGGCTAATGATTCACACGC
CGATGGACATCCTTCACAGGCGTATTTCACGTGGCGTACCTTTACTTCTGCCGGTAATCGACATGGTATGAGTCCGTGTGTTTTTATGACTATCGTCAGC
GTTGACCCTAATTTTGGTCGTCGGGTACGCAATCGCCGCCAGTTAAATAGCTTGCAAAATACGTGGCCTTATGGTTACAGTATGCCCATCGCAGTTCGCT
TGTATCTTTGGTTGTCGGTATATTGACCATCGAAATTCGCCGAGTGGAAATCGTAGTTGTCCGGTGTTGGTTGGTCTTGCACTTTTCGCAGGACGCACA
GGCTAAATACGTTAACAAAAAGTCAGATATGGACCTTGCTGCTAAAGGTCTAGGAGCTAAAGAATGGAACAACTCACTAAAAACCAAGCTGTCGCTACTT
CGAACCATTCAACCTAATTCGTGAGGCACCTGTCTAAACAGTAACACTCGTAAAAGTAGGGCTTCAACGCCGAGTAAGACTAAGACTTGTFGAAGAACCC
TGGGTTACGACGCGACGCCGTTCAACCAGATATTGAAGCAGAACGCAAAAAGAGAGATGAGATTGAGGCTGCGAAAAGTTACTGTAGCCGACGTTTTGGC
ACGTCCAACCTATGCGGTTAGTAAAAATAGCTTCGCGCGTATTTAAACTCGTCTAAACAGCAGTGTCCAACGCGG
```

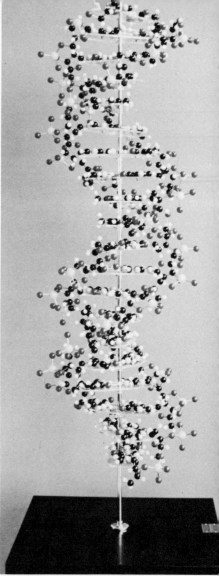

*Above: J.D. Watson and his famed model of the DNA molecule.
Left: this is the genetic code of an extremely
small virus. Roughly a million pages of this
type would be needed to show the genetic code
that is embodied in a single cell of a mammal.*

tiny segment of a chromosome and contains hundreds of genes. What did it look like? Like a curving, twisting ladder, or spiral staircase, now known as the *DNA double helix.*

Crick and Watson also made experiments that helped prove conclusively that DNA contains the genes that determine a person's heredity. *It is the number, arrangement, and kinds of units in DNA that determine a person's genetic code.*

DNA acts like a computer. It regulates all activities needed to keep the body healthy and growing at a normal rate. The bone cells, for example, are "told" by DNA to keep growing until a child becomes an adult. If a bone breaks, DNA will "tell" the bone cells to make new cells to heal the break.

One of the amazing facts about the genetic code is its structural similarity in all living things. In every case, however, this "computer bank" does different things for different species. You won't see a plant with eyes, for example. Nor will you see boys or girls with leaves growing on their bodies. The genetic code for humans can produce only human traits. But all genetic codes have a similar structure and work similarly in reproducing and maintaining a species.

RNA

The nucleus of each cell, which contains DNA organized into chromosomes, also contains *proteins.* Every protein has a different purpose. Some help nourish the cell and keep it healthy. Others make it possible for the cell to reproduce. Still other proteins help determine such things as how fast a person will grow or how well he or she will resist disease. Proteins cannot reproduce themselves, however. New proteins are formed only by the DNA reproducing itself.

DNA does not act alone in producing proteins, however. It is assisted by three kinds of ribonucleic acid (RNA): *mes-*

senger RNA, transfer RNA, and ribosomal RNA. First, messenger RNA makes a copy of one strand of DNA. Transfer RNA then sets up a matching strand in the proper order. Ribosomal RNA then acts to hold the new DNA strands together, which then become the new source of protein in meeting the body's needs.

MORE ABOUT CHROMOSOMES

Each and every species on earth has its own number of chromosomes. But there is no relation between chromosome number and the complexity of an organism. Human beings have forty-six chromosomes in each cell. Some one-celled animals and other simple organisms have several hundred.

Sex cells, or cells that are used to create a new member of the species (also called gamete cells), have only half the number of chromosomes found in body cells—in humans, twenty-three. The gamete cell in a woman is called the ovum, or egg. The egg is produced by two small organs in the female called the ovaries. In a man the gamete cell is the sperm. Sperm are produced by the male organs known as the testicles. When a man's sperm cell penetrates a woman's egg, fertilization takes place. The nucleus of the egg and the nucleus of the sperm unite to form a single nucleus that has forty-six chromosomes, twenty-three from the mother and twenty-three from the father. The new cell is known as a zygote. By mitosis, other cells are produced, and growth begins, leading to the birth of a child.

Determining Sex
The forty-six chromosomes in each body cell are arranged in pairs, so as to form the double strand helix mentioned earlier. In a female, each pair of chromosomes has the same general

[33]

The human chromosomes

X Y

| 1 | 2 | 3 | 4 | 5 | 6 | 7 |

| 8 | 9 | 10 | 11 | 12 | 13 | 14 |

| 15 | 16 | 17 | 18 | 19 | 20 | 21 | 22 |

shape. But in the male, the twenty-third pair is a bit more unusual. These are the chromosomes that determine a child's sex. In women, the sex chromosomes are both shaped like X's, and are thus usually identified by scientists as XX. But in men, one sex chromosome is shaped like an X and the other like a Y, and is thus known as the XY chromosome. The male sperm (which always contains *only one* of the two possible chromosomes) may contain an X chromosome or a Y chromosome. Thus, if a child is born female, this means she has inherited an X chromosome from each parent. If a child is born male, he has inherited an X chromosome from his mother and a Y chromosome from his father. In addition, the boy or girl inherits twenty-two other pairs of chromosomes, one pair from each parent.

[34]

SEX-LINKED TRAITS

Some traits other than sex are passed on in the sex cells of the mother or father, the X and Y chromosomes just discussed. For this reason they are called sex-linked traits. *Color blindness* is a good example. The most common form of this condition is an inability to distinguish red from green. The condition is caused by a recessive gene carried on the X chromosome. The trait shows up only when there is no dominant gene for normal vision to override it.

Color blindness shows up most often in males. This is because males inherit only one X chromosome. (From the mother. The other sex chromosome they inherit is a Y from the father.) If the defective gene for color blindness is on the mother's X chromosome, the condition will show up. A female, on the other hand, inherits *two* X chromosomes—one from each of her parents. Even if one of the X chromosomes carries the defective gene, chances are the other will carry the gene for normal color vision. Since the gene for normal vision is dominant, the defect won't show up, and the girl won't be color blind. However, if her pair of genes for color vision include both dominant and recessive traits, she can pass the trait on to her offspring, particularly the males.

Hemophilia, or bleeder's disease, is another sex-linked trait. Like color blindness, it is also caused by a defective recessive gene carried on the X chromosome. Hemophiliacs are known as bleeders because their blood cannot coagulate (thicken) and form a scab over a wound to stop it from bleeding. Thus, when hemophiliacs wound themselves, they are liable to bleed to death. Hemophilia is a very serious condition, and only very recently has any real progress been made in helping hemophiliacs survive.

GENOTYPE AND PHENOTYPE

Whenever scientists study the genetic makeup of humans, they try to determine if the differences are inherited or if they are the result of reactions to the environment. A study of the family history of each parent, going back many generations, will help to reveal a person's *genotype*.

Your genotype includes all the genes (trait determiners, dominant and recessive) you have inherited. Your *phenotype* is revealed in your appearance: your hair, the shape of your nose, your eyes, how tall you are, and so on. These traits are the result of combinations of genes, both dominant and recessive, discussed earlier. There may be many recessive genes in your genetic code that have not shown up. They are still there in your chromosomes. When you marry and have children, some of these may show up, depending on what new combinations of genes result when your children are conceived.

FIND-OUT-FOR-YOURSELF Project 4: Talk with your parents about traits you may have inherited from them and from their parents.

1. Make a list of your observable traits (your phenotype), those that you and your parents are aware of.
2. Make a list of other traits you may have inherited that have not shown up yet but may show up later in your life.
3. Make a list of other traits you may have inherited from your parents and grandparents (your genotype) that may not show up in you but may be passed on to your children.
4. Study your brothers and sisters and make lists of their phenotypes.

Record in a notebook all the information obtained.

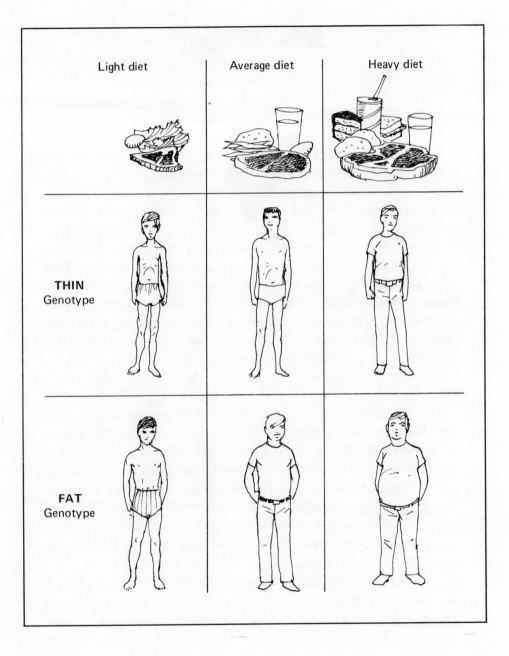

MUTATION

CHAPTER
9

Darwin understood how plant and animal life evolved over long periods of time. The fittest survive. Those traits that made them the fittest were passed on to their offspring.

Darwin also tried to explain how a completely new species could suddenly appear, one that was quite different from its parents in one or more ways. He tried to explain this by his theory of variation, but failed to prove anything scientifically.

New forms of life that sprang up suddenly were generally known as *mutations,* from the Latin word *mutare,* which means to change. One of the first scientists to record experiments in which mutations were actually developed was Hugo De Vries, a Dutch scientist from Amsterdam. After experimenting with many plants, De Vries decided to use a variety of Lamarck's Evening Primrose to test his theories.

From this one variety De Vries was able to observe in his gardens several new forms. One new form had a smooth leaf rather than the crinkly leaf of its parents. Another had red streaks in its seed pod. On one new plant the leaves were a very dark green and denser than the parent plants. And one was a dwarf plant, about half as big as its parents. But

Hugo deVries

the flowers were just as big as the parent plants had been. Later studies showed that some of the new types of plants were not true mutations but the result of hereditary traits already present in the parent plants. In all, however, De Vries recorded more than a dozen mutations in his studies of the primrose.

It was De Vries who established the fact that mutations are *not* the result of gradual variations in traits inherited from parents (new combinations of hereditary material). Nor are they caused by changes in the environment. They just suddenly "happen."

Long before scientists conducted experiments to show how mutations could develop, many people were aware of the phenomenon. In 1791 in Massachusetts, for example, a farmer named Seth Wright found a sheep among his flock that had short legs and a sagging back. This made it difficult for the sheep to jump fences and wander off or get lost. Aware of this advantage, Farmer Wright began to breed the new sheep so he could have more like it. This is how the famous breed known as Ancon sheep developed.

About a century later, in 1889, a farmer in Atchison, Kansas, found that one of his Hereford cattle hadn't grown any horns. This was an advantage because it made the animal more peaceful and less likely to injure other cattle. The breed developed from this mutation became known as polled (hornless) herefords.

Many scientists since De Vries have experimented with

This albino raccoon, found in Illinois in 1975, is the only such mutation ever found.

plants and animals to find out more about mutation. One of the commonest forms of animal life used in heredity experiments for a long time was the tiny fruit fly known to scientists as *Drosophila.* In one series of mutation experiments, scientists used a fruit fly that had red eyes, a gray body, and long wings.

What kinds of mutations developed? Quite a variety! There were flies with white eyes, flies with yellow bodies, flies with wings so small they couldn't fly, and flies whose eyes were not fully developed.

White robins, guinea pigs with pink eyes, waltzing mice, and thousands of other mutants have been identified since Darwin's time. Many experiments have proved the fact that mutants occur naturally in all plant and animal life. But it has only been in recent times that scientists have discovered anything about *how* mutations occur.

Mutations happen when the sequence of units in DNA gets disrupted. This can happen when one unit is substituted for another. It can also happen if a new unit is added to the DNA strand, or if one of the units is imperfectly formed (if it is larger than it should be, smaller, or has one part missing). Only if the mutation occurs in the sex cell (the gamete), however, will the change be passed on.

What causes these changes? Certain chemicals and overexposure to radiation have been found to cause mutations, both in body and in sex cells. But there are probably many other as yet undiscovered causes. Scientists are hard at work now trying to find out more about the mutation phenomenon.

HEREDITY AND ENVIRONMENT

CHAPTER
10

Which is more important in determining what you look like, environment or heredity? How intelligent you are? How healthy you are and how long you will live? How important you will be to your family, friends, other people, the world?

These are some of the questions that were asked when scientists began to debate the relative importance of heredity and environment.

Mark Twain, a famous American humorist and author, wrote most of his books in the last half of the nineteenth century. This was during the time of Mendel and Darwin. One of his books, called *The Prince and the Pauper,* is the story of two look-alikes, Tom Canty, a poor boy who liked to pretend that he was a prince, and the Prince of Wales, who later became England's King Edward VI. They meet and exchange clothes and identities, each pretending to be the other. The story tells how well they succeed in fooling people. But in the end they go back to being who they were.

This makes for a good story. But it is not scientifically possible. Look-alikes are not identical twins. And it is impossible that they could have inherited exactly the same physical traits. Nor could their voices and mannerisms be the same. Even if heredity caused them to look the same, environment would have made them different.

But which is more important in determining what a person will be like when he or she grows up, heredity or environment? Darwin's cousin, Sir Francis Galton, believed heredity was. In a book he wrote in 1869 called *Hereditary Genius,* Galton described the family histories of several famous Englishmen and their ancestors. In each case he showed how each generation produced "eminent" men. The reason for this, concluded Galton, was heredity. These families passed on to each new generation of offspring the intelligence and physical health that led to achievement.

At that time, this attitude may have appeared to be true. Wealthy families could afford to give their children the best of all opportunities to succeed in life. They could send them to college. And they could arrange for them to have important jobs. Children born into the poorer classes remained poor and had little opportunity to become wealthy or hold important jobs.

In 1875 an American scientist named R. L. Dugdale made a study of a group of families whom he called the "Jukes." He traced this family from colonial times to his own time. Among the descendants he found 222 criminals and more than 200 paupers. A few decades later, another study was made by H. H. Goddard of a family he called the "Kallikaks." He traced this family back to someone he called "the Old Horror." This man's descendants included 143 children who were born feeble-minded, 24 who became alcoholics, and 66 criminals and other individuals of questionable character.

The reason that the Jukes and the Kallikaks were such failures, many scientists argued, was because of their heredity, their "bad" genes. In the struggle for existence, these scientists said, people with good genes will overcome disadvantages. People born with bad genes will always be bad.

But at the same time other scientists were saying that environment was more important in determining what an individual grew up to be. These scientists blamed society, which allowed poverty and ignorance, the seedbed of crime, to exist. It had nothing to do with what the children had inherited from their parents. Give them enough good food to eat, clothing to wear, a good education, and a good understanding of right and wrong, the scientists said, and the children will become good members of society and not turn to crime as a way of life.

To try to solve this dilemma, many scientists have conducted tests to study the effects of environment on heredity. They have found that some inherited traits cannot be changed by environment. Blood type is a good example. There are just four blood types among humans: O, A, B, and AB. Each of us is born with one of these. Giving a person a transfusion using a blood type different from his or her own might cause death.

Scientists now know, however, that neither heredity nor environment alone is solely responsible for a person's character. True, a child of the Juke or Kallikak family, who grows up among criminals and people living in poverty, is more than likely to follow his or her parents' bad example. But there are many cases of people who have overcome the obstacles of poverty and ignorance, and gone on to achieve great things in business, science, and other professions. So many examples of this were documented that in time scientists concluded that *both* heredity and environment were important, and that neither can be singled out as *the* determining factor in how a person turns out.

TWINS

When a mother gives birth to two babies at the same time, the babies are called twins. Sometimes they are *identical* twins. Identical twins come about because the mother's egg divides into two parts after it has been fertilized by the father's sperm. Each develops into a separate individual from the union of one egg and one sperm. Because each twin inherits the same genes, they are born "identical."

Sometimes twins are born who are not identical. In this case, two separate eggs have been fertilized by two different sperm. Two children are born, but they are completely different individuals, and are known as *fraternal* twins. They are as different from each other as if they had been born at different times.

Identical twins are always of the same sex. Fraternal twins can be of the same sex too. But they can also be of different sex.

Studies have been made of identical and fraternal twins to find out how closely they resemble each other physically and in their character traits, and how they are different. Identical twins will have the same hair and eyes, the same kind of nose and other physical features. But fraternal twins can be quite different. One may more closely resemble the father, the other the mother.

The same similarities and differences are seen in the tendency toward certain diseases. Tuberculosis, a disease caused

A twins' club in Pittsburgh, Pennsylvania.
Twins occur in approximately
one out of every eighty-seven births.
Only one-quarter of these are identical.

by a germ that invades the lungs, bones, and other parts of the body, used to be one of the most dreaded diseases in the world. Now there are medicines and treatments that can cure it. This disease is not inherited. It is in the environment. But some people are more likely to get the disease than others. They are more *genetically conditioned* to fall victim to the disease because of the physical traits they have inherited from their parents.

The ability to resist certain diseases or overcome them is inherited. And when one identical twin has this capability, in most cases, so does the other twin. This is true because they have inherited exactly the same traits from their parents.

Studies have also been made of the intelligence of identical and fraternal twins. Scientists are quick to point out, however, that how a child responds to the environment is important in estimating how intelligent he or she is. Even among identical twins there are differences in how each twin responds to the environment. Many factors are involved, including encouragement from parents, the opportunity to learn, and the quality of the child's education.

Studies have also been made of the character traits of twins. For instance, scientists wanted to find out if the tendency to become a criminal was inherited. In the case of identical twins, they found that if one twin was a criminal, it was more than likely that the other twin would be a criminal too.

They also studied twins to find out if the tendency to smoke cigarettes and develop lung cancer was inherited. They reached the same conclusions. If one identical twin smoked and developed lung cancer, it was more likely that his or her co-twin would also.

In all of these studies, however, scientists found that the environment in which the twins lived was *more* important than heredity. When children grow up in an environment in which crime is an accepted way of life, they are more likely to become criminals. Children who grow up in a family or an area in which it is considered wrong to commit crime are more likely to be law-abiding citizens. And people who smoke are more likely to get lung cancer, whether they are twins or not.

Environment makes a big difference in whether a boy or girl grows up to be a Juke or a Kallikak rather than one of the eminent men Lord Galton talked about. What you inherit from your parents does not determine your character. No one is a born criminal or a born heavy smoker. What your environment is and how you respond to it is just as important in determining what kind of person you will grow up to be.

FIND-OUT-FOR-YOURSELF Project 5: Plant the same variety of bean in different environments.

1. Fill two flower pots with garden soil.
2. In one pot sprinkle a small amount of fertilizer and mix it with the soil. (Suggestion: use an all-purpose fertilizer.) Do not add fertilizer to the second pot.
3. Plant two bean seeds in each pot, following the directions on the package.
4. Place the pots on a windowsill that gets sun most of the day. Water each pot twice a week.
5. After the seeds have sprouted, measure each plant at two-week intervals until they are fully grown (about six weeks after sprouting).

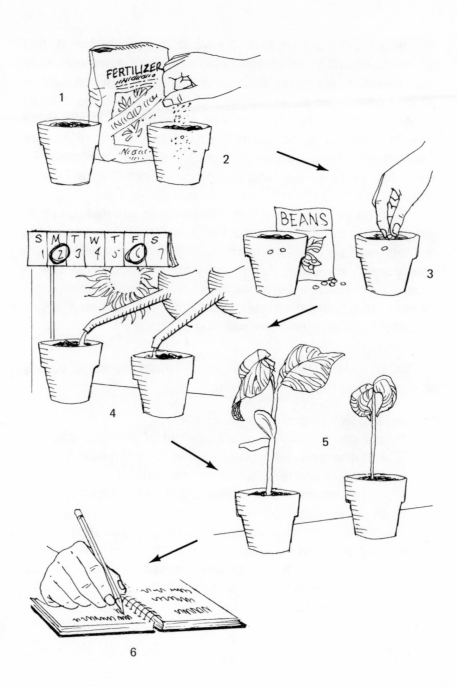

6. Record the growth rate of each plant in a notebook. Also note the difference in the appearance of the plants when they are fully grown.

CONTROLLING HEREDITY

CHAPTER
11

Some scientists believe that in time it may be possible to control many of the traits a person may inherit. They believe they will be able to do this by changing the genes in a person's body or by changing the environment in which he or she happens to live. The science that explores the possibility of changing genes to make a person healthier is known as *genetic engineering.* The science that explores the possibility of changing the environment in order to achieve the same purpose is called *environmental engineering.*

HEREDITARY DISORDERS

There are many inherited disorders passed on by the genes. Some of these have already been touched on earlier in our discussion of sex-linked traits. Many inherited disorders can be treated. For example, one of the most serious diseases a child can be born with is retinoblastoma, or cancer of the eye. This is caused by a dominant gene inherited from one or both parents. Until recently, this disease was fatal unless the afflicted eyes were removed. This saved the child's life, but left him or her blind. Doctors now sometimes use a technique called cryosurgery in which the diseased part of the

[52]

eye is destroyed by freezing it. The frozen portion is then removed, leaving the rest of the eye in place and still able to function.

New research in medicine is making it possible to treat other genetic defects successfully. A rare disease called galactosemia is caused by a recessive gene inherited from both parents. The child is born without an enzyme in his or her genetic code that makes it possible to digest milk. This can result in liver damage, mental retardation, convulsions, and even death. But if the disease is discovered soon enough, the galactose, or milk sugar that causes the problem, is eliminated from the child's diet.

A more common inherited disease is diabetes, or the inability of a person's body to produce a substance known as insulin. Diabetes is believed to be caused by a combination of two recessive genes, one inherited from each parent. The disease is not necessarily fatal, but it can cause serious physical problems and lead to heart disease. Now, people who have diabetes get insulin from external sources.

Another well-known genetic defect is nearsightedness. A person with this disease can see clearly at short distances but not at long distances. Treatment for this problem is to wear glasses.

The cures for many of the foregoing defects are found in a person's environment. What science has not been able to do is to change a person's genes. Much research today, however, is concerned with the possibility of doing this.

Among those working on this kind of research are *geneticists,* men and women scientists who specialize in the study of genes. They try to find out how genes are inherited, how they affect a person's life, both physically and mentally, and how they respond under different environments. A leading geneticist of recent times, Theodosius Dobzhansky, declared: "If mankind succeeds in improving genetics, genetics may succeed in improving mankind."

MOLECULAR GENETICS

One of this century's greatest scientific advances was the discovery of the genetic code. This led to a new branch of the science of heredity called *molecular genetics,* the study of genes found in chromosomes and how to control them. It is called molecular genetics because it concentrates on the smallest unit in the DNA substance, the DNA molecule.

Scientists have discovered, for example, that the genes found in the chromosomes of a cell nucleus are not always active. Something causes these genes to be switched on and off. Scientists are now trying to find out if they can switch off genes that are causing harm to the body and switch on genes that keep the body healthy.

Other studies are being made of how to replace defective or missing genes with healthy genes. This has already been done in experiments with bacteria. Scientists have taken the DNA from one kind of bacteria and implanted it in another bacteria, giving it new, healthy genes to replace those that were missing or defective. The same thing has been done with human cells, but not in living human beings.

Recombinant DNA

In another experimental area the DNA from two completely different organisms, such as mammals and bacteria, are being combined to form new kinds of life. One purpose of these *recombinant DNA* experiments is to create organisms for the manufacture of hormones such as insulin and other helpful medicinal substances, including antibiotics.

The techniques developed for use in recombining DNA

molecules have also made it possible for scientists to remove sections of chromosomes containing a number of genes with known functions from various forms of animal life. The detached section of the chromosome is then reattached to a growing organism such as bacteria. As the bacteria grows, it reproduces the altered DNA segment many times, allowing scientists to study it in greater detail. This process is called *molecular cloning* (from the Greek word *klon,* which means twig or shoot, as in a tree or bush that grows many identical twigs or branches).

Some people have become alarmed at these experiments. They are afraid that some of the new and strange organisms might escape from the laboratory and be harmful to human life and other animals as well as to plants. For this reason, very strict rules have been developed for conducting genetic research to make it as safe as possible.

Cell research in general holds great promise because so many mental and physical illnesses originate in the cell. Even though science has unlocked some of the mysteries of the genetic code, many questions have yet to be answered.

No one yet knows what causes a cell to die, for instance. If they knew the answer, scientists might be able to slow the aging process so we could live longer, healthier lives. In time, by solving more mysteries of the genetic code, we may be able to change it so that no one will inherit any mental or physical defects or have to suffer the tragedy of cancer.

Someday, perhaps, geneticists may be able to show us how to replace worn-out or diseased tissues. Perhaps they will find a way to make amputated arms or legs grow back. The same hope applies to plants and livestock. Improving their hereditary chances will result in higher food production to feed a hungry world.

[55]

WHO YOU ARE, WHAT YOU WILL BE

CHAPTER
12

Until you are an adult, you can't know just how tall you are going to be. If you're light-haired now, maybe your hair will get darker, be more like Uncle Fred's hair or Aunt Mary's. And right now you can't be sure exactly what your nose will look like.

You may not like school very much now, or find many of the subjects interesting. Then again, maybe you will later, when you have a better idea of what you want to do when you grow up.

You have lots of time to think about these things. Your heredity—all the characteristics you have inherited—will make a difference. So will your environment, and how you respond to it. Your parents and friends, and the teachers at school will influence you. In fact, just about everything you see and hear or understand in the world around you will make a difference.

A lot of what happens depends on you. Some things you can't change, but others you can. It is up to you to make the most of what you have inherited and the opportunities you find in the world around you.

GLOSSARY OF IMPORTANT TERMS

cell—the smallest unit of an organism that is capable of functioning independently. It consists of a nucleus surrounded by cytoplasm, various organelles, and proteins.

chromosomes—rod-like structures composed of units called genes, found in the DNA in living cells. DNA in humans is made up of forty-six chromosomes (twenty-three pairs).

DNA—deoxyribonucleic acid, a substance found in the nucleus of a living cell, organized into bodies known as chromosomes. It is usually found in a double strand made up of a series of units called genes.

environmental engineering—ways of making changes in the environment to make it a better and healthier place in which to live.

evolution—the theory that all living things, plants and animals, change over the course of time.

fertilization—the result when a male sex cell unites with a female sex cell to produce a new plant or animal.

fraternal twins—two children who are born at the same time from the union of two different eggs and sperm.

gametes—the sex cells in human beings (the sperm in the male and the ova in the female). Each gamete cell has twenty-three chromosomes, only half the number found in other body cells.

genes—the units in the chromosomes that contain the dominant and recessive traits.

genetic code—all the genes a living organism has inherited. They determine an organism's appearance and how it functions, grows, and maintains itself.

genetic engineering—ways of controlling heredity by replacing missing or defective genes with healthy genes (still only a possibility).

geneticists—scientists who specialize in the study of genes and heredity.

genotype—all the traits, both dominant and recessive, that a child has inherited from his or her parents.

heredity—the traits that are passed on to offspring by parent plants and animals.

hybridization—the cross-fertilization or breeding of plants and animals that have one or more different traits.

identical twins—two children born at the same time from the same egg and sperm, thus inheriting identical traits.

mitosis—the process by which a cell makes a new cell which is an exact copy of itself.

molecular genetics—the study of DNA molecules to identify the form and function of genes contained therein.

mutation—a plant or animal with a completely new trait that has not been inherited.

natural selection—the theory that all living things are subject to variation and survival of the fittest.

nucleus—the part of each living cell that contains the hereditary material.

ovum (or egg)—the female reproductive cell produced by organs called ovaries in plants and animals.

phenotype—all of the observable traits a person has inherited.

pistil—the female part of a plant that contains the ovary.

pollen—a powdery substance produced by the male part of a plant (the stamen).

pollination—the act of transferring the pollen from the male part of a plant (the stamen) to the female part (the pistil).

proteins—substances found in all living cells that nourish the cell, keep it healthy or repair it, and make it possible for a cell to make new cells. Certain proteins called enzymes speed up chemical reactions. Some hormones, substances that regulate chemical activities in the body, are proteins. So are the antibodies that help your body fight disease.

recombinant DNA—a technique in which genes from two different organisms are joined together to form new kinds of life.

RNA—ribonucleic acids found in the nucleus of a living cell which make it possible for the cell to reproduce itself.

sperm—male reproductive cells in humans and other animals.

stamen—the male part of a plant.

survival of the fittest—the hereditary process by which traits are passed on to offspring that make it possible for them to survive in a particular environment.

variation—the theory that no two living organisms are exactly alike. (Identical twins are identical at birth but slight changes usually develop as they grow older, in response to their environment.)

zygote—the new cell formed when the man's sperm unites with a woman's egg during fertilization.

[59]

A CHRONOLOGY OF MAJOR EVENTS IN THE SCIENCE OF HEREDITY

1655   *Robert Hooke of Britain* designed his own microscope to study tiny particles of matter. He discovered that they were made up of units he called cells.

1801   *Jean Baptiste Lamarck of France* published his theories of evolution. This included the belief that all life forms change over the course of time. But he was unable to prove this scientifically.

1838   *Matthias Schleiden of Germany* published the cell theory as applied to plants.

1839   *Theodor Schwann of Germany* published the cell theory as applied to animals.

1859   *Charles Darwin of Britain* proved the scientific basis for evolution in his book, *The Origin of Species.*

1865   *Gregor Mendel of Austria* announced his theories of heredity, which have become known as Mendel's Laws.

1869   *Sir Francis Galton of Britain* published a book, *Hereditary Genius,* in which he claimed heredity alone was responsible for a person's character traits.

1869   *Friederich Miescher of Switzerland* discovered DNA.

1875 *R. L. Dugdale of the United States* published his study of the "Jukes" family whose descendants included many criminals and paupers.

1900 *Hugo De Vries of the Netherlands, Carl Correns of Germany, and Erich Tschermak of Austria,* each working independently of the other, rediscovered Mendel's work.

1901 *Hugo De Vries* published his findings on mutations, which just suddenly "happen."

1902 *Walter S. Sutton of the United States* announced that during cell division the chromosomes act as Mendel had suggested.

1907 *Thomas Hunt Morgan and Alfred H. Sturtevant of the United States* and other biologists at Columbia University in New York discovered that genes (trait determiners) are located on the chromosomes.

1912 *H. H. Goddard of the United States* published his study of the "Kallikak" family, many of whose descendants were feeble-minded, alcoholic, or criminal.

1927 *Hermann J. Muller of the United States* produced mutations through the use of X-rays.

1941 *George W. Beadle and Edward L. Tatum of the United States* discovered that genes control the production of enzymes (proteins that speed up all chemical reactions in the body, such as turning food to fuel).

1944 *Oswald T. Avery of the United States* announced that DNA and DNA alone was the substance responsible for heredity.

1953 *Francis H. C. Crick of Britain and James D. Watson of the United States* made a model of the DNA molecule, known as the DNA double helix. They also proved conclusively that genes determine a person's heredity.

1953   *Arthur Kornberg of the United States* showed that DNA could reproduce outside of a cell.

1955   *Severo Ochoa of Spain* created RNA.

1957   *Arthur Kornberg* produced DNA in a test tube.

1966   Discovery of the genetic code.

1967   *Arthur Kornberg* produced DNA that was *biologically active* (able to reproduce naturally).

INDEX

DATE DUE